Ten Essential Vocabulary Strategies

Practice for Success on Standardized Tests

Book 4
Lee Mountain

Educators Publishing Service
Cambridge and Toronto

Acquisitions/Development: Sethany Rancier
Cover Design: Karen Lomigora
Typesetting: Sarah Rakitin
Editor: Mary Troeger
Managing Editor: Sheila Neylon

Copyright © 2004 by Educators Publishing Service, a division of Delta Education, LLC.
All rights reserved. No part of this book may be reproduced or utilized in any form or by any electronic or mechanical means, including photocopying, without permission in writing from the publisher.

ISBN 0-8388-3023
Printed in U.S.A.

Contents

Becoming a Word Whiz: What's in It for Me? — v

Unit 1. The Top Ten Types of Vocabulary Test Questions — 1

    1. Meaning in Sentence and Passage — 2
       Practice for Success — 3

    2. Context Clues — 5
       Practice for Success — 6

    3. Best Words for Blanks — 8
       Practice for Success — 9

    4. Multiple Meanings — 11
       Practice for Success — 12

    5. Dictionary Information — 14
       Practice for Success — 16

    6. Figurative Language, Featuring Similes and Metaphors — 17
       Practice for Success — 19

    7. Synonyms and Antonyms, Featuring the Importance of Context — 21
       Practice for Success — 22

    8. Affixes and Roots, Featuring Prefixes of Number and Quantity — 24
       Practice for Success — 25

    9. Word Relationships — 27
       Practice for Success — 28

    10. Pairings, Featuring Text and Graphics — 30
       Practice for Success — 32

Unit 2. Practice Test Passages with Vocabulary Questions — 34

    1. Fiction: "The Strength of a Sled Dog" from Jack London's
       The Call of the Wild — 35
       Vocabulary Questions — 35

    2. Autobiography: "Speech without Sight or Hearing"
       from Helen Keller's *The Story of My Life* — 38
       Vocabulary Questions — 39

3. Informational Article: Central-American Tree Spinach	42
Vocabulary Questions	42
4. Anecdote: "'Run Faster,' Cried the Queen" from Lewis Carroll's *Through the Looking Glass*	45
Vocabulary Questions	46
5. Classic: "A Place and a Person" from Washington Irving's *The Legend of Sleepy Hollow*	49
Vocabulary Questions	49
6. Essay: The Test of Time	52
Vocabulary Questions	53
7. Content-Area Material: The Sea Anemone	56
Vocabulary Questions	57
8. Beliefs: Martin Luther King Jr.'s Support of the Poor	59
Vocabulary Questions	60
9. Graphics and Wordplay: Popular Puzzles	62
Vocabulary Questions	63
10. Pairings: Gwendolyn Brooks and Phyllis McGinley, Two Poets Who Won Pulitzer Prizes	66
Vocabulary Questions	67
Unit 3. More Practice on Vocabulary through Wordplay	71
1. The Stronger Synonym	72
2. Idioms, Featuring Wacky Wordies	73
3. Ana-Pal Pairs	75
4. Double Definitions	76
5. Analogy Puzzle	78

Becoming a Word Whiz: What's in It for Me?

Have you ever tried to lift an unabridged dictionary? It is one of the heaviest books in the library. It aims to list and define ALL the words in our language. Even after college, you will not know all those words.

But the more dictionary definitions you know, the better off you are as a reader. Despite that fact, the dictionary is probably *not* the first place you turn when you are reading and you meet a new word. When you are in the middle of a good book, you are seldom willing to stop to look up a word. That would interrupt the flow of your reading.

Probably you use the dictionary only when no other vocabulary strategy works. You first try to figure out the new word by looking at its context, the words around it, to check for clues to its meaning. Or you might look within the word, at its root and affixes, for meaning clues. Then, too, you might look "between the lines and beyond the lines" for clues to figurative meaning.

In all your reading, you use such strategies to unlock the meanings of words. But you make special use of vocabulary strategies when you take a test. Strategies for figuring out new words help you to do your very best on the test, especially with words that are on the fringe of your vocabulary.

It's easy to answer test questions about words that are fairly familiar. But it takes skill to get at the meaning of a word you know only slightly. You will develop that skill as you work through this book. With *Ten Essential Vocabulary Strategies* at your disposal, you can become a test-wise word whiz.

Test day is important—yes. But you read on thousands of other days too. On all those days you meet new words, and you need to unlock meanings. So you will benefit every day, as well as test day, from using *Ten Essential Vocabulary Strategies*.

Unit 1
The TOP TEN
types of vocabulary test questions

There are many ways to design questions about words. On tests, each question usually leads to four multiple-choice answers. But you need to use different strategies on different types of vocabulary questions, even if their wording is similar. Here are ten types of questions that are used on tests:

1. Meaning in sentence and passage
2. Context clues
3. Best words for blanks
4. Multiple meanings
5. Dictionary information
6. Figurative language
7. Synonyms and antonyms
8. Affixes and roots
9. Word relationships
10. Pairings

It is a big plus to know a strategy for handling each of these ten types of vocabulary questions. If you use the right strategy for each type, you will do well on tests.

A smart test taker reads a question about a word, and then rereads the sentence or the paragraph in which the word appears. Rereading helps you focus on the word in context, that is, the words around it that determine its meaning. Sometimes you need to reread more than just one sentence. Sometimes the whole paragraph contributes to the context. Though you use context to some degree in answering most vocabulary items, you need a different strategy for each of the top ten types of questions.

Let's look at the types, one by one. First, you'll see an example of each, with the answer explained in the "Think Aloud" section. Then you'll do "Practice for Success" exercises on test questions of that type. To conclude each lesson, there is an "Explain the Strategy" section, in which you will tell in your own words how you approach that type of vocabulary question.

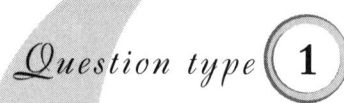

Meaning in Sentence and Passage

What should you do when you meet an unfamiliar word early in a paragraph? Read on! See if the meaning of the word becomes clearer to you. By the time you reach the end of the paragraph, you may have picked up a lot of meaning clues.

Example

> The verbivores arrived. In they walked, ready for their club meeting at school. They were carrying dictionaries, crossword-puzzle books, Scrabble games, thesauruses, and wordplay magazines. These lovers of language would spend the next hour having fun with words. That's what verbivores do.
>
> Which meaning best fits the word *verbivores*?
>
>   A. students who go to club meetings
>
>   B. students who carry dictionaries
>
>   C. students who enjoy language play
>
>   D. none of the above

Think Aloud

The first sentence of the preceding paragraph gives you very little help with the word *verbivores*. The second sentence gives much more help. It suggests that *verbivores* are students who belong to a school club. The third sentence lets you know what materials *verbivores* bring to their meetings. The fourth sentence makes it clear that the club members know how to have a good time. By the time you meet *verbivores* again at the end of the paragraph, you have figured out the meaning of the word.

Be careful not to be tricked by the first two answers, A and B. They are incomplete. They could apply to many other students. Yes, *verbivores* do go to club meetings, but so do students who are not *verbivores*. Yes, *verbivores* do carry dictionaries, but so do students who are not *verbivores*. Their enjoyment of language (they absolutely eat it up) is what sets *verbivores* apart. So answer C is the best fit.

Practice for Success
Meaning in Sentence and Passage

1. The librarian's helpers were efficient. They shelved the returned books in the right spots. They kept the records straight at the check-out desk. They never wasted time, and they did all of their jobs well. The librarian said that having efficient helpers was important.

    Which meaning best fits the word *efficient*?

    A. educated

    B. prompt

    C. effective

    D. attractive

2. She decided on her priorities. First, she'd complete her homework. That was tops in importance because she wanted good grades. Second, she'd clean up her room. Mom insisted on that. Third, she'd phone Aunt Sarah. That could wait until tomorrow. Setting priorities helped her put first things first.

    Which meaning best fits the word *priorities*?

    A. numbering of items

    B. lists of things to do

    C. rankings in order of importance

    D. private ideas

3. The house was dilapidated. Most of the paint had peeled off the door. Two window shutters were missing, and most of the glass panes were cracked. The roof sagged. The place had a sorry appearance.

   Which meaning best fits the word *dilapidated*?

   A. falling apart

   B. ready to be repaired

   C. needing paint

   D. occupied

4. If only she could be completely exonerated, thought Angela. Then people would stop whispering behind her back, staring at her, still wondering. The not-guilty verdict in court had set her free. But the burden of proving her absolute innocence was still with her. If only people could know she was totally blameless!

   Which meaning best fits the word *exonerated*?

   A. freed from all suspicion

   B. wishing for better treatment

   C. lifted out of anger

   D. comforted in sadness

5. His appearance was slovenly. No comb or brush had been near his hair. Gravy drippings dotted the front of his jacket. His shirttail was hanging out. No one sat next to him on the bus.

   Which meaning best fits the word *slovenly*?

   A. dusty

   B. uncaring

   C. lazy and sleepy

   D. untidy and dirty

Explain the Strategy
Meaning in Sentence and Passage

Suppose you meet an unfamiliar word in the first sentence of a paragraph. What should you do to unlock its meaning?

_____

_____

_____

Question type 2
Context Clues

You know from the preceding lesson that sometimes it takes a whole paragraph to build the context for a new word. Other times, however, one or two words provide such strong hints that they make the meaning of a new word jump out at you.

Test makers may ask you to identify these strong context clues. Remember, this type of question does NOT ask for the meaning of a word. Instead it asks you to identify the surrounding words that lead you to the meaning.

Example

The leafy philodendron will grow rapidly indoors in wet soil.

Which context clues lead you most directly to the meaning of *philodendron*?

    A. *leafy* and *soil*
    B. *the* and *grow*
    C. *will* and *indoors*
    D. *in* and *rapidly*

Think Aloud

As soon as you see the word *leafy*, you register a strong context clue. Anything *leafy* is in the plant category. When you see the word *soil* at the end of the sentence, you notice another strong context clue. Wet *soil* is good for plants. By the time you finish the sentence, you know that a philodendron is a plant. The context clues make the meaning clear to you.

Would you expect to find "plant" among the answers? No. This question does not ask you for the meaning of the word *philodendron*. It asks you for the context clues that lead you to the meaning.

It is easy to reject three of the four answers because they contain general words like *the*, *will*, and *in*. These cannot be strong context clues because they do not lead you directly to the meaning of another word. So the only answer that works is the first one, "A. *leafy* and *soil*."

Practice for Success
Context Clues

1. In the dense fog, even the people across the street were completely invisible to us.
   Which words are the context clues that lead you to the meaning of *dense*?

    A. *fog* and *invisible*

    B. *people* and *us*

    C. *street* and *across*

    D. *completely* and *even*

   What do you think *dense* means? _____

2. Moving stealthily through the trees, the Komodo dragon sneaked up on its unsuspecting prey.
   Which words are the context clues that lead you to the meaning of *stealthily*?

    A. *dragon* and *prey*

    B. *through* and *its*

    C. *trees* and *moving*

    D. *unsuspecting* and *sneaked up on*

   What do you think *stealthily* means? _____

3. The strings of the guitar vibrated when she plucked them with her fingers.
   Which words are the context clues that lead you to the meaning of *vibrated*?

   A. *her* and *with*

   B. *plucked* and *strings*

   C. *the* and *guitar*

   D. *she* and *them*

   What do you think *vibrated* means? _____

4. On the archery range, she lifted the bow, carefully aimed the arrow at the target, and hit the bull's-eye.

   Which words are the context clues that lead you to the meaning of *archery*?

   A. *range* and *hit*

   B. *bow* and *arrow*

   C. *carefully* and *target*

   D. *aimed* and *lifted*

   What do you think *archery* means? _____

5. Before starting the operation at the hospital, the surgeon checked his instruments.
   Which words are the context clues that lead you to the meaning of *surgeon*?

   A. *the* and *before*

   B. *his* and *checked*

   C. *hospital* and *operation*

   D. *instruments* and *starting*

   What do you think *surgeon* means? _____

Explain the Strategy
Context Clues

Suppose you meet a test question that asks you to find the specific context clues that lead to the meaning of a particular word. How do you approach such a question?

_____

_____

Practice for Success on Standardized Tests

Question type

Best Words for Blanks

When you are reading a book, you never encounter a blank in the middle of a sentence. All the words are shown. The text is complete.

On a test, however, you may be asked, "What is the best word for the blank?" or "What are the best words for the two blanks?" This type of question tests your comprehension. It asks you to use the words around the blanks to figure out what word or words would do the best job of completing the sentence.

Example

> She wore a _____ coat because it was a _____ day.
>
> Which pair of words fits best in the blanks?
>
>   A. *red* and *windy*
>
>   B. *heavy* and *cold*
>
>   C. *light* and *freezing*
>
>   D. *new* and *sunny*

Think Aloud

In a question with two blanks, there is often a relationship between the words. It may be a comparison or a contrast. It may be cause and effect. It may suggest a progression or another type of relationship. Let's figure out the relationship in this sentence, "She wore a _____ coat because it was a _____ day."

Did you spot the word *because* in the middle of the sentence? It gives you a strong clue about the type of relationship. The word *because* is a signal of cause and effect. The weather caused her to wear a certain kind of coat. What kind of coat and what kind of weather?

With answer A, it would be a *red* coat because of the *wind*. No. Wind does not cause the choice of the color red.

With answer B, it would be a *heavy* coat because it was *cold*. That makes sense. Cold weather does cause people to wear heavy coats.

With answer C, it would be a *light* coat because of *freezing* weather. Wrong. Choosing a light coat on a freezing day makes no sense.

With answer D, it would be a *new* coat on a *sunny* day. There is no relationship between *new* and *sunny*. Clearly, answer B is the best choice.

Practice for Success
Best Words for Blanks

1. In order to weigh _____ he knew he should exercise _____ .
   Which words fit best in the blanks?

    A. *daily* and *weekly*

    B. *less* and *more*

    C. *down* and *up*

    D. *early* and *late*

2. She finished summer _____ , took a trip, and then fall _____ started.
   Which words fit best in the blanks?

    A. *training* and *growing*

    B. *books* and *library*

    C. *homework* and *vacation*

    D. *school* and *classes*

3. When Mom heard the _____ alert, she said we should leave the _____ .
   Which words fit best in the blanks?

    A. *shark* and *water*

    B. *attic* and *tornado*

    C. *pool* and *mountains*

    D. *hurricane* and *garage*

4. The swimmer needed to increase his _____ to keep from being cut from the _____ .

   Which words fit best in the blanks?

   A. *speed* and *team*

   B. *stroke* and *squad*

   C. *dive* and *relay*

   D. *turn* and *meet*

5. He practiced tap dancing every _____ , so he was ready to _____ in the recital.

   Which words fit best in the blanks?

   A. *week* and *demonstrate*

   B. *month* and *sing*

   C. *period* and *fail*

   D. *day* and *perform*

Explain the Strategy
Best Words for Blanks

On a test you may be asked to choose the best pair of words to fill two blanks. How would you approach this type of question?

_____

_____

_____

Question type 4
Multiple Meanings

Suppose you were asked, "What is the meaning of the word *score*?" Many people would say something like this: "The *score* is the number of points made by one team against another." That's often the first meaning that comes to mind, but it is not the only definition of *score*. There are many others. Some may not be familiar to you.

Watch out when you meet a test question about a seemingly easy word like *score*. The familiar answers can lead you to make too quick a choice.

Example

> We liked the lively score for the movie so much that we decided to buy a CD of the sound track.
>
> In the sentence above, what is the meaning of the word *score*?
>
> A. points in a game
>
> B. grade on a test
>
> C. twenty
>
> D. music for a production

Think Aloud

Score is a word with multiple meanings. The dictionary lists all four of the meanings above, and quite a few others besides. No doubt you know the first two: "A. points in a game" and "B. grade on a test." They are familiar, but in this sentence neither makes sense. If you jump to select one of them, you will be wrong.

The third answer, "C. twenty," might make you think of the first line of the Gettysburg Address, which starts, "Four score and seven years ago." But nothing in the sentence above shows a connection with the number twenty.

Maybe you need to stretch your thinking to a less familiar meaning of the word. The last answer, "D. music for a production," may seem unfamiliar at first glance. But think. The sentence says we are buying the sound track because we like the score. The only answer that has any connection to *sound* is *music*. Therefore, the last answer is the best choice.

Practice for Success
Multiple Meanings

1. The ladies in hoopskirts hired a coach to take them to the theater.
   In the sentence above, what is the meaning of the word *coach*?

    A. trainer of a sports team

    B. private tutor

    C. large horse-drawn carriage

    D. low-priced seating area on a plane

2. With great effort, he broke his nail-biting habit.
   In the sentence above, what is the meaning of the word *broke*?

    A. smashed

    B. brought to an end

    C. proved false

    D. cut open the surface

3. She held the title to all fifty acres of the farm.
   In the sentence above, what is the meaning of the word *title*?

    A. rank

    B. name

    C. championship

    D. claim or right

4. There is no craft in the smile of an infant.
   In the sentence above, what is the meaning of the word *craft*?

   A. practiced skill in making

   B. artistic handwork

   C. ship or plane

   D. falseness or cunning

5. He decided to stall for time, hoping help would arrive soon.
   In the sentence above, what is the meaning of the word *stall*?

   A. delay cleverly

   B. put into a section of a stable

   C. come to a stop without meaning to

   D. bring to a halt

Explain the Strategy
Multiple Meanings

Suppose you meet a vocabulary question in which all four answers are real definitions of the word. How do you select the correct answer?

_____

_____

_____

Question type 5
Dictionary Information

You already know how to use the dictionary for help with a word's spelling, part of speech, and meaning. But test makers expect you to know how to use all parts of a listing. They frequently ask you to choose the definition that best fits the context of a sentence or passage. You know that if you determine what part of speech the word is in a sentence, then you can find its meaning more quickly. The dictionary separates definitions by parts of speech.

Test makers may ask about phonetic spellings, the spellings with marks that show the pronunciation. Or they may ask about the meaning of the word when it is used in a special phrase. Both of these items are included in the dictionary listing. You just need to know where to look.

The phonetic spelling comes right after the word and is in parentheses or brackets. If the word is used in any special phrases, such as idioms or familiar expressions, these appear after the definitions.

In the following listing of the word *throw*, note the phonetic spelling in parentheses. In this word, the line over the *o* shows that the letter is pronounced with the long *o* sound. (The marks that are used to show pronunciation are usually listed at the bottom of the dictionary page with explanations.)

Note that if a word has any other forms, these will be given next. Here the past tense of *throw* is irregular. It does not form the past tense by adding the letters *ed*. So the dictionary includes the forms *threw* and *thrown*. After giving the definitions for the word, the listing then gives several phrases that *throw* is part of (*throw away, throw in, throw off,* and *throw over*) with their definitions.

Example

> **throw** (thrō) **threw, thrown** v. 1. to move or send rapidly. 2. to lose a game or fight deliberately. n. 1. a pitch or toss. 2. a lightweight cover used for a sofa or bed. **throw away** 1. to discard. 2. to waste. **throw in** 1. to add extra or free. 2. to join with. **throw off** 1. to recover from. 2. to mislead. **throw over** 1. to give up or abandon. 2. to jilt.
>
> The thief planted false clues, hoping to throw off the police.
>
> Which set of definitions helps you with *throw off* in the sentence above?
>
>   A. verb definitions
>
>   B. noun definitions
>
>   C. phrase definitions
>
>   D. none of the above

Think Aloud

Your first step is to reject the first two answers, the verb and noun definitions of *throw*. The question asks you about *throw off*.

At the end of the dictionary listing you find the definitions for the different phrases *throw* is part of that have a new meaning.

The two definitions of *throw off* show you its meanings. "To recover from" does not make sense in the sentence, but the other definition, "to mislead," works perfectly. You choose C as the best answer.

This is just one of many forms that dictionary questions can take on tests. You will see others in the following "Practice for Success" items.

Practice for Success
Dictionary Information

To answer these questions, look back at the dictionary listing of *throw*.

1. They used a colorful throw to hide the tear in their couch.
   Which definition fits the word *throw* as it is used in the sentence above?

   A. the first verb definition

   B. the second verb definition

   C. the first noun definition

   D. the second noun definition

2. If you make 89 points on the test, the teacher will throw in one point to get you up to 90. Which definition helps you with *throw in*, as used in the sentence above?

   A. to move or send rapidly

   B. to lose a game deliberately

   C. to add extra

   D. to join with

3. The phonetic spelling of the word *throw* is thrō. The line over the letter o is called a macron. It means that the letter o is pronounced with the long sound, which is the same as the name of the letter. Which of these words would be spelled phonetically with a macron over the letter *o*?

   A. how

   B. town

   C. tow

   D. cow

4. You are writing a sentence using *throw* to talk about *yesterday's* baseball game. You want to be sure you are spelling the word correctly. Which of these spellings would the dictionary listing of *throw* give you?

   A. through

   B. threw

   C. thorough

   D. three

5. At the carnival, Patricia *threw away* all her money, trying to win a prize in one of the booths. Use the dictionary information to help you decide which adjective below describes Patricia.

    A. wasteful

    B. unthinking

    C. happy

    D. tired

Explain the Strategy
Dictionary Information

Suppose a vocabulary question includes a dictionary listing. What kinds of information can you get from the listing?

_____

_____

_____

Figurative Language
Featuring Similes and Metaphors

Test questions may ask you to determine the meaning of different kinds of figurative language. First, try to decide what kind of figurative language is used and then work on narrowing down the answers to the most likely one.

Figurative language comes in many forms. As you know, an idiom is an expression whose meaning is different from the meaning of the individual words. Sensory words require you to use your senses to see, hear, feel, taste, and smell what the author is conveying. Similes and metaphors are forms of figurative language that use comparisons. In a simile, the comparison is stated, as in "fast *as* the wind" or "*like* a slow boat." A metaphor, on the other hand, is suggested by identifying two things or activities as the same in order to suggest they share some of the same qualities. For example, "His *stomach* was such a *bottomless pit* that he wanted a third helping of dessert."

Practice for Success on Standardized Tests 17

Look at the following lines from the poem *Evangeline* by Henry Wadsworth Longfellow.

> *Example*
>
> This is the forest primeval.
>
> The murmuring pines and the hemlocks,
>
> Bearded with moss and in garments green,
>
> Indistinct in the twilight,
>
> Stand like the Druids of old.
>
> What is the poet describing when he writes, "bearded with moss and in garments green"?
>
> A. children walking in the forest
>
> B. tall trees
>
> C. breezes murmuring through the forest
>
> D. low bushes

Think Aloud

In these lines of poetry, you may not be familiar with the words *primeval, indistinct,* or *Druids.* Such difficult words may make you want to give up on the question. But don't give up! You can work around the vocabulary difficulty. You can think your way through to the correct answer.

Start by focusing on the one line, "bearded with moss and in garments green," which is quoted in the question. Look at the nouns in the four answers—*children, trees, breezes, bushes.* Which noun is most likely to be "bearded with moss and in garments green"?

You can reject "A. children walking in the forest" because the words *children* and *bearded* just don't belong together. Also, there is no suggestion of youth or children in the lines. On the contrary, the poem suggests that the forest is old.

It's easy to reject "C. breezes murmuring through the forest," even though the word *murmuring* appears in the poem. *Breezes* are not concrete enough to be "bearded with moss and in garments green."

The other two answers, "B. tall trees" and "D. low bushes," could both have "garments green" because of their leaves and needles. But "bearded with moss" suggests enough height to have moss hanging. So bushes are probably too low. You have thought your way through to "B. tall trees" as the most likely answer.

To check your reasoning, reread the lines. You notice that in line 2, the words *pines* and *hemlocks* refer to trees. This verifies your answer. Take a look at the following items that show you some test questions relating to figurative language.

Practice for Success
Figurative Language

1. A single shrub covered with snow stood like a solitary ghost beside the road. What feeling is conveyed by the simile in the preceding sentence?

    A. fright

    B. sadness

    C. joy

    D. loneliness

2. While his pursuers poked around his hiding place, he lived a year of terror in a minute. What does the figurative language in the preceding sentence suggest?

    A. His pursuers caught him.

    B. He had fought with his pursuers.

    C. He had found a good hiding place.

    D. He was terrified of being caught.

3. They peered into the dense darkness, but it was like trying to see through a thick blanket. What does the simile in the preceding sentence suggest?

    A. It was twilight.

    B. It was the middle of the night.

    C. The darkness was pitch black and unbroken.

    D. In the darkness, someone was covered by a heavy blanket.

4. Donne wrote, "No man is an island, entire of himself; every man is a piece of the continent, a part of the main."

   What did Donne mean by his metaphors?

   A. Each person stands alone.

   B. Each island is part of a continent.

   C. All people are connected.

   D. People should not live on islands.

5. The director knew the project could fail if this big-name star was not handled with kid gloves.

   What is the meaning of the idiom, "handled with kid gloves"?

   A. treated with special tact and care

   B. supplied with children's mittens

   C. given gloves made of goatskin

   D. dealt with directly

Explain the Strategy
Figurative Language

When you spot figurative language in a test item, how can you think your way through to the correct answer?

_____

_____

_____

Question type 7
Synonyms and Antonyms Featuring the Importance of Context

As you know, antonyms are words that are opposite in meaning. But if a word has several meanings, it can also have antonyms for each of those meanings. For example, take the word *light*. *Light* and *dark* are antonyms, and so are *light* and *heavy*. You need to read the word *light* in context to know whether its antonym is *dark* or *heavy*. Whenever you answer a test question about an antonym, you need to consider its part of speech and the context before you decide what its antonym is.

Example

> Because they needed peace and quiet, the couple spent the summer at their retreat by the lake.
>
> What is the antonym of *retreat*, as the word is used in the sentence above?
>
> A. advance
>
> B. silent home
>
> C. restful cottage
>
> D. noisy house

Think Aloud

The first answer, "A. advance," is very tempting. You are looking for an antonym of *retreat*. Certainly *retreat* and *advance* are opposites. But is *advance* the antonym of *retreat* as *retreat* is used in the test sentence? Let's reread the sentence: "Because they needed peace and quiet, the couple spent the summer at their retreat by the lake." In that sentence, *retreat* is a noun, probably a place to live. So *advance* does not fit.

The second and third answers sound like synonyms of *retreat*, " B. silent home" and "C. restful cottage." The second and third answers trick as many readers as the first answer. They get confused and mark a synonym (a word with a similar meaning) rather than an antonym.

But you are a careful reader. So you'll think, "In that particular sentence, *retreat* means 'a quiet place to stay.'" There is really only one possible antonym among the answers. It's "D. noisy house."

As you know, test questions on synonyms often ask you to choose among shades of meaning. For synonyms, just as for antonyms, you need to reread the sentence in which the word appears. Context can help you figure out shades of meaning for synonyms, just as it helped you with the antonyms.

Practice for Success
Synonyms and Antonyms

1. He grew so rapidly that the pants he bought in March were too short by May.

    What is the antonym of *short*, as the word is used in the preceding sentence?

    A. tall

    B. long

    C. brief

    D. shrunk

2. When the salesperson claimed one amazing quality after another for the washing machine, I began to question her truthfulness.

    Which synonym of *question* best fits the way the word is used in the preceding sentence?

    A. ask

    B. speak

    C. inquire

    D. doubt

3. Farmers living in northern latitudes labor from dawn to dusk to make use of their short summers.

   What is the antonym of *dusk*, as the word is used in the preceding sentence?

   A. twilight

   B. sunset

   C. daybreak

   D. dust

4. Because he was tardy, he missed the morning announcements.
   Which synonym of *tardy* fits the way the word is used in the preceding sentence?

   A. unpunctual

   B. overdue

   C. belated

   D. prolonged

5. The ascent of Mount Everest is a challenge, even for the best of climbers.
   What is the antonym of *ascent*, as the word is used in the preceding sentence?

   A. description

   B. descent

   C. lowering

   D. scaling

Explain the Strategy
Synonyms and Antonyms

In test items about synonyms and antonyms, why should you carefully check the part of speech and context of the featured word?

_____

_____

_____

Question type **8**

Affixes and Roots
Featuring Prefixes of Number and Quantity

Sometimes you can find clues to meaning *around* a new word. At other times, you can find the meaning *within* the word itself. A familiar prefix, root, or suffix may help you determine its meaning.

Let's look at some meaningful prefixes that are related to numbers and quantities. You know that a unicycle has one wheel, and a bicycle has two wheels. *Uni-*, and *bi-* are meaningful parts of other words too. To unify is to bring together as *one*. To bisect is to cut in *two*. Some prefixes that suggest number or quantity are *multi-, macro-, maxi-, mini-,* and *micro-*. As you probably know, the first three suggest *many* or *large* and the last two mean *few* or *small*.

On tests you often need to look *within* a new word for clues to its meaning. You may find a meaningful part that will help you figure out the right answer.

Example

After his injury, Jason was incapable of marching in the parade to celebrate the town's centennial.

What is the meaning of the word *centennial*?

A. July 4

B. one hundred years

C. landmark

D. human rights

Think Aloud

You know from context that *centennial* refers to some occasion for celebration. But all four answers fit with parades and celebrations. How can you narrow down the answers? Look inside the word *centennial*. You see *cent* at the beginning. What other words do you know that start with *cent*? *Centipede*, perhaps? That creature looks like it has a hundred legs. Or, from your math textbook, do you remember *centimeter*? That unit of measure is equal to 1/100 of a meter. Of course, you know the word *century* with its "hundred" connection. As these associations race through your mind, you probably zero in quickly on the second answer, "B. one hundred years." You looked inside the word to get your strongest clue.

Practice for Success
Affixes and Roots

1. Since she was bilingual, she did an excellent job of interpreting for us on our trip. How many languages did she speak?

    A. one

    B. two

    C. three

    D. four

2. It will take a multipurpose tool to complete all parts of the job. Which words best describe a *multipurpose* tool?

    A. many uses

    B. large parts

    C. great idea

    D. finished job

3. At the airport, we had minimal problems going through the different checkpoints before boarding the plane.

   How many problems did we have?

   A. none

   B. a great number

   C. the least to be expected

   D. the usual number

4. He has been studying only half an hour each evening, but in order to pass, he must *quadruple* his study time.

   According to the sentence above, how long should he study each evening from now on?

   A. half an hour

   B. one hour

   C. two hours

   D. four hours

5. The fence was covered with multiflora roses.
   Which of the following would you expect these plants to have?

   A. many roots

   B. lots of flowers

   C. large stems

   D. gigantic leaves

Explain the Strategy
Affixes and Roots

How can a familiar affix or root help you figure out the meaning of a word?

_____

_____

_____

Question type **9**

Word Relationships

In the lower grades, you probably worked with analogies like "*See* is to *eyes* as *hear* is to *ears*." The word relationships in that analogy are hard to miss. You see with your eyes, and you hear with your ears.

At your grade level, however, the analogies in your textbooks and on your tests are not so easy. They can be tricky. You may need to figure out the relationship of the words in greater detail. The first step in solving an analogy is to put the first pair of words into a sentence that expresses the relationship between them. For example: You see with your eyes. To determine the missing word in the second part, you need to find a word that will fit the same sentence. You hear with your _____. In some analogies, making a sentence will solve the analogy. But in other analogies you need to look for more precise areas of similarity.

Example

Complete this analogy:

Foot is to *sock* as

   A. *hand* is to *glove*

   B. *leg* is to *pants*

   C. *hand* is to *mitten*

   D. *arm* is to *sleeve*

Think Aloud

You can begin by making a sentence to express the relationship between the two terms. "A foot is covered by a sock." But you soon see that all the answers name a part of the body and a covering for that part of the body. So you need to go a step further to read them for the fine points. How closely does each one relate to "*foot* is to *sock*"?

The first answer, "A. hand is to glove," looks good at first glance. "*Foot* is to *sock* as *hand* is to *glove*" seems correct. But you want to look at the other answers, just to make sure that the first answer shows the most exact relationship.

There is something troubling about "B. leg is to pants." A pair of pants has two legs. So the relationship is almost, but not quite, right.

The third answer, "C. hand is to mitten," makes you take another look at your previous choice, "A. hand is to glove." Is a sock more like a mitten or a glove? A glove has a separate part for each finger. Does a sock have a separate part for each toe? No. So a sock is more like a mitten.

Notice that in the analogy both *foot* and *sock* are singular—one foot and one sock. That fact helps you reject "D. arm is to sleeves," since *sleeves* is plural. You have looked for the answer that has the closest relationship with "foot is to sock." You have thought your way through to "C. hand is to mitten" as the best choice. And it is.

There are many formats for analogy questions. Some may require only one step. But others will take two steps like the preceding example. Still other analogy questions may ask you to identify the type of relationship between the words, such as matching words that are the same part of speech. As you know, not all word-relationship questions are analogies. You may also be asked to spot connections based on sound, spelling, or context.

Practice for Success
Word Relationships

1. Complete this analogy:
   Four is to *parallelogram* as *eight* is to _____ .

   A. *pentagon*

   B. *rhombus*

   C. *diamond*

   D. *octagon*

2. Complete this analogy:
   City is to *state* as *mayor* is to _____ .

   A. *president*

   B. *governor*

   C. *representative*

   D. *senator*

3. Complete this analogy:
   Bat is to *flying* as

   A. *ball* is to *hitting*

   B. *throwing* is to *pitcher*

   C. *worm* is to *crawling*

   D. *monkey* is to *swing*

4. *Word* is to *sentence* as *paragraph* is to *essay*.
   In the analogy above, what is the relationship between the words?

   A. part to whole

   B. cause to effect

   C. older to younger

   D. shape to number of sides

5. Complete this analogy:
   Forward is to *backward* as

   A. *stop* is to *pots*

   B. *brag* is to *garb*

   C. *spin* is to *nips*

   D. all of the above

Explain the Strategy
Word Relationships

When you meet an analogy on a vocabulary test, how do you think your way through to the correct answer.

_____

_____

_____

Question type

Pairings
Featuring Text and Graphics

When you read, you need to understand graphics as well as you do text. You meet graphics (diagrams, tables, charts, maps, and pictures) in newspapers, magazines, books, and on tests. A test question may require you to get information about a topic from a pair of sources. In the following example, you will look for information in a paragraph and in a bar chart.

Example

Speeds of birds, beasts, and fish are hard to compare. As a rule, flying is faster than running, and running is faster than swimming, but there are exceptions. A house cat can run faster than a blue jay can fly. A sea turtle can swim about twenty miles per hour, but a land turtle's speed is about one tenth of a mile per hour. A rabbit can run faster than a greyhound—but only for a few minutes. The greyhound can continue its speed for a longer time. At track meets, a distance runner cannot maintain the speed of a sprinter. And although the following bar chart shows twenty miles per hour as the speed for human beings, this rate is only possible with training.

How rapidly can a rabbit run for a brief period of time?

    A. twenty miles per hour

    B. thirty miles per hour

    C. forty miles per hour

    D. more than forty miles per hour

30 . . . . .Ten Essential Vocabulary Strategies

Estimated Rates of Speed for Different Creatures

Creatures	Speed in miles per hour (10–60)
Blue jay	~20 (Flying)
Human being	~20 (Running)
Sea Turtle	~20 (Swimming)
Robin	~30 (Flying)
House cat	~30 (Running)
Sailfish	~30 (Swimming)
Owl	~40 (Flying)
Greyhound	~40 (Running)
Dragonfly	~50 (Flying)
Gazelle	~50 (Running)
Hummingbird	~60 (Flying)

KEY: Flying, Running, Swimming

Think Aloud

As you think about this question, you may decide to look at the chart first, hoping to see *rabbit* listed in the column at the left. No luck! The word *rabbit* is not in the list. You remember, however, that a rabbit is mentioned in the paragraph.

Back to the paragraph. Quickly you skim through the lines and find this sentence: "A rabbit can run faster than a greyhound—but only for a few minutes." That helps, if you know how fast a greyhound can run.

Back to the bar chart. Is *greyhound* listed? Yes. What is the estimated speed for a greyhound? According to the chart, it's forty miles per hour.

Now to the question once again. "How rapidly can a rabbit run for a brief period of time?" Faster than a greyhound. So the answer, "D. more than forty miles per hour," looks like the best choice. You have put together information from two sources, the paragraph and the chart, to figure out the answer.

The pairing of a paragraph with a graphic such as this one is not the only type of grouping you will meet on tests. Sometimes you answer vocabulary questions about an illustration and the text related to it. Other times you are asked to compare and contrast material about two people. You will see examples of many different kinds of questions that might be asked about two sources.

Practice for Success
Pairings

Use the preceding bar chart and paragraph to answer these questions.

1. The title of the chart is "Estimated Rates of Speed for Different Creatures." In this context what is the meaning of *estimated*?

    A. exact number

    B. number based on some evidence

    C. random number based on guesswork

    D. personal opinion

2. Both the chart and the paragraph give you information about the speed of a human being. Which speed?

    A. swimming

    B. running

    C. both of the above

    D. neither of the above

3. The paragraph gives information about the speeds of both the land turtle and the sea turtle. Which speed is shown in the chart?

    A. swimming

    B. running

    C. both of the above

    D. neither of the above

4. You met the word *exceptions* in the paragraph. Which of the following sentences states an *exception*, as the word is used in the paragraph?

   A. A dragonfly is faster than a greyhound.

   B. An owl is faster than a sailfish.

   C. A gazelle is faster than a sea turtle.

   D. A sailfish is faster than a blue jay.

5. The key to the preceding bar chart shows three shades of gray for three activities. What does the darkest shade stand for?

   A. flying

   B. running

   C. swimming

   D. crawling

Explain the Strategy
Pairings

On tests you will meet questions that pair two sources of information, such as a paragraph and a chart. How do you approach such questions?

_____

_____

_____

Practice for Success on Standardized Tests

Unit 2

Practice TEST PASSAGES
with vocabulary questions

You will read many kinds of passages on tests. Then you will answer vocabulary questions about them. Here are the kinds of passages you will use as practice tests in this book.

1. Fiction
2. Autobiography
3. Informational article
4. Anecdote
5. Classic
6. Essay
7. Content-area material
8. Beliefs
9. Graphics and Wordplay
10. Pairings

Throughout these practice tests, you will meet the top ten types of vocabulary questions. Following each question is the name and number of its type. Sometimes two types (or strategies) are equally helpful in figuring out an answer. In these cases, two numbers are given.

If you have trouble with a question, turn back to its pages in Unit 1. Then try again. You will probably be able to figure out the correct answer.

Ten multiple-choice questions follow each practice test passage. Working with many different kinds of questions about varied reading selections will help you think strategically about meanings, no matter what you are reading.

1. Fiction: THE STRENGTH OF A SLED DOG
adapted from the novel *The Call of the Wild* by Jack London

The miners were boasting about their favorite sled dogs. "My dog can <u>start</u> a sled with a load of five hundred pounds and walk off with it," said one. Another man <u>bragged</u> that his dog could pull six hundred pounds. Matthewson, the richest of the miners, claimed seven hundred pounds for his dog.   1

John Thornton boasted, "My dog Buck can <u>start</u> a sled with a thousand pounds. He's the best in Alaska."   2

"Can he break the _____ out of the ice and pull it a hundred yards?" _____ Matthewson.   3

"Buck can do it," John Thornton said <u>coolly</u>.   4

"Well, I've got a thousand dollars that says he can't," Matthewson stated slowly, so that all could hear. So saying, he slammed a sack of gold dust down on the bar. Nobody spoke.   5

John Thornton's <u>bluff</u>, if it was a <u>bluff</u>, had been called. He could feel a flush of warm blood creeping up his face. His tongue had tricked him, boasting about his dog. He did not know if Buck could pull a thousand pounds. Half a ton! The thought of it frightened him.   6

Vocabulary Questions

1. Which words in the first sentence of this passage give you context clues about the characters and the setting?

    A. *miners* and *sled dogs*

    B. *boasting* and *the*

    C. *favorite* and *were*

    D. *about* and *their*

    Question type **2**: **Context Clues**

2. Which synonym of the underlined word *bragged* best fits the way it is used in paragraph 1?

    A. declared

    B. rejoiced

    C. triumphed

    D. boasted

    Question type **7**: **Synonyms and Antonyms**

3. Which definition best fits the way the underlined word *start* is used in paragraphs 1 and 2?

   A. begin a project

   B. introduce

   C. move from a stationary position

   D. enter someone into a game

Question type (4): **Multiple Meanings**

4. In paragraph 3, what are the best words for the blanks?

   A. *sled* and *asked*

   B. *dogs* and *said*

   C. *pounds* and *told*

   D. *miner* and *inquired*

Question type (3): **Best Words for Blanks**

5. What is an antonym of the underlined word *coolly* as it is used in paragraph 4?

   A. friendly

   B. excitedly

   C. coldly

   D. fiery

Question type (7): **Synonyms and Antonyms**

6. Which word from paragraph 5 makes the strongest impact on your sense of hearing?

   A. stated

   B. hear

   C. slammed

   D. spoke

Question type (6): **Figurative Language**

7. In paragraph 6, which context clues enable you to figure out the weight of a *ton*?

   A. *thousand pounds* and *half*

   B. *Buck* and *could pull*

   C. *frightened* and *bluff*

   D. *boasting* and *tricked*

   Question type 2 : **Context Clues**

8. Complete this analogy:
   Ton is to *weight* as

   A. *light* is to *brightness*

   B. *ocean* is to *depth*

   C. *kilometer* is to *distance*

   D. *measurement* is to *inch*

   Question type 9 : **Word Relationships**

9. Here is a dictionary listing for the word *bluff*.

   bluff (bluf) n. 1. a high steep bank or cliff. 2. a false bold front. v. 1. to impress by using false confidence. 2. to mislead or deceive.

   Which dictionary definition of *bluff* is closest to the meaning of the word as it is used in paragraph 6?

   A. the first noun definition

   B. the second noun definition

   C. the first verb definition

   D. the second verb definition

   Question type 5 : **Dictionary Information**

Practice for Success on Standardized Tests 37

10. In the last paragraph, you read this sentence: "He could feel a flush of warm blood creeping up his face." What does this mean?

   A. He was bleeding.

   B. He was blushing.

   C. He was creeping.

   D. All of the above

Question type 6 : **Figurative Language**

2. Autobiography: SPEECH WITHOUT SIGHT OR HEARING adapted from *The Story of My Life* by Helen Keller

1 When I was ten years old, I learned to speak! Before I lost my sight and hearing at the age of nineteen months, I had started to learn to talk. But after my illness I <u>ceased</u> to speak because I could not see or hear.

2 By the time I was seven, I could read a few easy books in raised print, thanks to my teacher. Also I could write on a Braille slate. But I could communicate as others do in speaking only by spelling with my fingers. One who is entirely dependent upon the <u>manual</u> alphabet has always a sense of <u>restraint</u>, of narrowness, of silence. So I resolved that I would learn to speak aloud.

3 My teacher's <u>method</u> was this: she passed my hand lightly over her face, and let me feel the position of her tongue and lips when she made a sound. I was _____ to imitate every motion, and in an hour I had _____ six elements of speech: M, P, A, S, T, I.

4 I shall never forget the surprise and delight I felt when I <u>uttered</u> my first connected sentence, "It is warm." True, they were broken and stammering syllables, but they were human speech. No deaf child who has earnestly tried to speak the words which he has never heard—to come out of the prison of silence, where no tone of love, no song of bird, no <u>strain</u> of music ever pierces the stillness—can forget the thrill of surprise, the joy of discovery which came over him when he uttered his first word.

5 But it must not be supposed that I really learned to talk in a short time. At first, most people would not have understood one word in a hundred that I <u>uttered</u>. I labored night and day to <u>articulate</u> each syllable in each word clearly. My work was practice, practice, practice.

Vocabulary Questions

1. In paragraph 1, which word is an antonym of *ceased*?

    A. learned

    B. lost

    C. started

    D. speak

    Question type 7 : **Synonyms and Antonyms**

2. Which phrase in paragraph 2 provides context clues that lead you to the meaning of the underlined word *manual*?

    A. read a few easy books

    B. thanks to my teacher

    C. spelling with my fingers

    D. learn to speak

    Question type 2 : **Context Clues**

3. Complete this analogy:
   Helen Keller is to *Braille* as a *sighted reader* is to

    A. textbooks

    B. print

    C. hearing

    D. speech

    Question type 9 : **Word Relationships**

4. In paragraph 2, what is the meaning of the underlined word *restraint*?

    A. being taught or educated

    B. restoring

    C. resting again

    D. being held back

    Question type 8 : **Affixes and Roots**

Practice for Success on Standardized Tests

5. Look at how the underlined word *method* is used in paragraph 3. Then complete this analogy:

   Method is to *teacher* as

   A. *preacher* is to *sermon*

   B. *cook* is to *recipe*

   C. *procedure* is to *scientist*

   D. *list* is to *shopper*

   ───── Question type 9: **Word Relationships** ─────

6. In paragraph 3, what are the best words for the blanks?

   A. *unable* and *mastered*

   B. *slow* and *lost*

   C. *hesitant* and *written*

   D. *eager* and *learned*

   ───── Question type 3: **Best Words for Blanks** ─────

7. Here is a dictionary listing for *strain*.

   strain (strān) n. 1. trace. 2. injury to part of the body. 3. short melody. 4. stress or force.

   Which dictionary definition fits the way the underlined word *strain* is used in paragraph 4?

   A. definition 1

   B. definition 2

   C. definition 3

   D. definition 4

   ───── Question type 2: **Context Clues** *and* ─────
   ───── Question type 5: **Dictionary Information** ─────

Ten Essential Vocabulary Strategies

8. In paragraph 4, reread the final sentence about the "prison of silence." When Helen Keller came out of the prison of silence, what could she do?

   A. hear

   B. speak aloud

   C. walk around freely

   D. leave her prison cell

   Question type (6) **:Figurative Language**

9. You meet the word *uttered* in paragraphs 4 and 5. As used by Helen Keller, what does *uttered* mean?

   A. talked rapidly

   B. gave speeches

   C. spoke aloud

   D. made sounds

   Question type (1) **:Meaning in Sentence and Passage**

10. In paragraph 5, what is the meaning of the underlined word *articulate*?

    A. pronounce

    B. shout

    C. practice

    D. succeed

    Question type (1) **:Meaning in Sentence and Passage**

3. Informational Article: CENTRAL-AMERICAN TREE SPINACH

At home you might hear, "Eat your spinach. It's good for you." Do you then gobble up your helping? Or do you resist this leafy low-to-the-ground vegetable, even though it has high <u>nutritional</u> merit? In this country we have a wide choice of foods, but we do not always eat what is good for us.   1

Throughout rural Central America, _____ choices are not as _____. For people in the country of Guatemala, not many kinds of green leafy vegetables are available. But they do have a native plant called chaya, or tree spinach, which is indigenous to the area. There, tree spinach leaves have long been part of the diet just as spinach is here. According to nutrition experts the leaves contain protein, fiber, some vitamins, and such <u>minerals</u> as calcium, phosphorus, and iron. The food value of tree spinach is similar to that of the spinach grown in North America.   2

Tree spinach, however, is unsafe for salads. Without cooking, the chaya leaves are toxic because they contain hydrocyanic acid. Although one minute of boiling destroys most of the acid, people usually take the <u>precaution</u> of boiling tree spinach for much longer.   3

Chaya was first introduced to the United States as a landscape plant. It is an attractive shrub, which grows to a height of about six to eight feet and thrives in well-drained soil. Some gardeners in Texas and Florida have <u>cultivated</u> it because their climate is suitable.   4

Slowly, however, chaya is becoming recognized as a food plant, too. When gardeners harvest the leaves for eating, they usually wear gloves because the young leaf stems have thin stingy spines. Chaya is prepared by chopping the leaves into small pieces and cooking them for about twenty minutes. Then they are served with butter. Enthusiasts <u>assert</u>, "Tree spinach is just as tasty as regular spinach, and just as good for you."   5

Vocabulary Questions

1. In paragraph 1 what is the meaning of the underlined word *nutritional*?

    A. tasty

    B. of value as food

    C. flavorful

    D. well cooked

Question type 1: **Meaning in Sentence and Passage**

2. Which words are best for the two blanks in paragraph 2?

   A. *food* and *wide*

   B. *drink* and *narrow*

   C. *spinach* and *broad*

   D. *plentiful* and *leafy*

   Question type 3 : **Best Words for Blanks**

3. Complete this analogy regarding two of the places mentioned in paragraph 2:

   Guatemala is to *Central America* as

   A. *city* is to *continent*

   B. *country* is to *region*

   C. *area* is to *county*

   D. *place* is to *boundary*

   Question type 9 : **Word Relationships**

4. Which sentence in paragraph 2 introduces *chaya* as another word for *tree spinach*?

   A. first

   B. second

   C. third

   D. fourth

   Question type 1 : **Meaning in Sentence and Passage**

5. Which context clues lead you to the meaning of the underlined word *minerals*, as it is used in paragraph 2?

   A. *vitamins* and *fiber*

   B. *calcium, phosphorus,* and *iron*

   C. *protein, nutrition,* and *food*

   D. *value* and *vegetables*

   Question type 2 : **Context Clues**

6. In paragraph 2 you meet the words *native* and *indigenous*. Here is a dictionary listing of *native*.

   native (nā' tiv) adj. 1. belonging to a region, indigenous. 2. inborn, natural. n. 1. a person born in a region. 2. a plant growing in a place naturally.
   What does this dictionary listing tell you about the words *native* and *indigenous*?

   A. They are antonyms.

   B. They are synonyms.

   C. They have a common root.

   D. None of above.

   Question type (5) : **Dictionary Information** *and*
   Question type (7) : **Synonyms and Antonyms**

7. In paragraph 3, what is the meaning of the underlined word *precaution*?

   A. talking ahead of time

   B. being cautious after eating

   C. promptness

   D. prevention of trouble in advance

   Question type (8) : **Affixes and Roots**

8. Which words from paragraph 3 are the context clues which make you aware that you could get sick from eating raw chaya?

   A. *contain* and *destroys*

   B. *leaves* and *salad*

   C. *acid* and *boiling*

   D. *unsafe* and *toxic*

   Question type (2) : **Context Clues**

9. In paragraph 4, what is the meaning of the underlined word *cultivated*?

   A. improved by training

   B. became familiar with

   C. sold as a crop

   D. helped to grow

Question type (4): **Multiple Meanings**

10. Which word is an antonym of the underlined word *assert*, as it is used in paragraph 5?

    A. claim

    B. deny

    C. fear

    D. resist

Question type (7): **Synonyms and Antonyms**

4. Anecdote: "RUN FASTER," CRIED THE QUEEN
   adapted from *Through the Looking Glass* by Lewis Carroll

Introduction

When you were younger, you read fables. Do you remember "Goat and Coyote," "The Country Mouse and the Town Mouse," and "The Wolf in Sheep's Clothing"? At the end of each fable was a short sentence that summed up the message of the story.

Like fables, some anecdotes also carry messages. But they don't include a sentence at the end to hammer home the message. They leave it to you to figure it out, as in this anecdote from Lewis Carroll's fantasy, *Through the Looking Glass*.

"Run faster," cried the Queen. "Faster, faster!" Then she and Alice ran so fast that they seemed to skim through the air. They hardly touched the ground with their feet. On and on they _____ , until Alice was quite out of _____ . Then, all at once, they stopped, and Alice found herself sitting on the ground. The Queen propped her up against a tree. "You may rest a little now," she said.   1

Alice looked around her in bewilderment. "Why, I do believe we've been under this tree the whole time. Everything's just as it was."   2

"Of course it is," said the Queen impatiently. "What did you expect?"

"Well, in my country," said Alice, "you'd get somewhere else, if you ran very fast for a long time, as we've been doing."

"A slow sort of country," said the Queen. "Now here, you see, it takes all the running you can do just to keep up, where you are. If you want to get somewhere else, you must run at least twice that fast."

Vocabulary Questions

1. Look at the underlined idiom "to hammer home" in the introduction. What does this expression mean?

    A. pound with a hammer

    B. emphasize strongly

    C. nail a paper to the wall

    D. take the hammer home

2. What is the meaning of the underlined word *message*, as it is used in the introduction?

    A. lesson, maxim

    B. note, letter

    C. e-mail, fax

    D. report sent between two persons

3. In paragraph 1, what is the meaning of the underlined word *skim*?

    A. to read hastily

    B. to remove floating matter from a liquid

    C. to glide swiftly over

    D. to throw a flat stone across water

4. Which words are best for the blanks in paragraph 1?

    A. *stopped* and *patience*

    B. *walked* and *smiles*

    C. *went* and *rest*

    D. *ran* and *breath*

Question type 3: **Best Words for Blanks**

5. Here is a dictionary listing of the word *prop*.

prop (prop) n. 1. a person or thing that gives support. 2. a pole placed against a structure. v. **propped, propping.** 1. to hold up. 2. to place or lean something or someone against a support.

Which definition fits the way the word in used in paragraph 1?

    A. the first noun definition

    B. the second noun definition

    C. the first verb definition

    D. the second verb definition

Question type 5: **Dictionary Information**

6. Which synonym of *bewilderment* best fits the way the word is used in paragraph 2?

    A. awe

    B. shock

    C. confusion

    D. wonder

Question type 7: **Synonyms and Antonyms**

7. What is the meaning of the prefix on the underlined word *impatiently* in paragraph 3?

   A. into

   B. against

   C. not

   D. toward

   Question type (8): **Affixes and Roots**

8. In paragraph 4, Alice talks about her country. What would be the best description of her country?

   A. a place in the real world

   B. a fantasyland

   C. a country ruled by the Queen

   D. a place ruled by Alice

   Question type (1): **Meaning in Sentence and Passage**

9. In paragraph 5, the Queen gives details of her country. What would be the best description of her country?

   A. a place where there is no need to run

   B. a place even more hurried than the real world

   C. a slow sort of country

   D. a country with many trees

   Question type (1): **Meaning in Sentence and Passage**

10. This passage is called an *anecdote*. Judging from the passage, which answer or answers help you define the word *anecdote*?

    A. a brief, interesting or humorous narrative

    B. a short speech

    C. a serious message

    D. none of the above

    Question type (1): **Meaning in Sentence and Passage**

5. Classic: A PLACE AND A PERSON
adapted from *The Legend of Sleepy Hollow* by Washington Irving

In the bosom of one of those spacious coves which indent the eastern shore of the Hudson River, there lies a little valley. It is one of the quietest places in the whole world. If ever I should wish for a place where I might <u>steal</u> away from the world and its distractions, I know of none more promising than this little valley. A drowsy, dreamy atmosphere seems to hang over the land.   1

In this valley there lived a schoolmaster. He was tall, but very thin, with narrow shoulders. He had long arms and legs, hands that dangled a mile out of his sleeves, and feet that might have served for shovels. His whole frame was most loosely hung together.   2

His head was small, and flat at the top, with huge ears, large green glassy eyes, and a long nose. To see him striding along the <u>profile</u> of a hill on a windy day, with his clothes <u>bagging</u> and fluttering about him, one might have <u>mistaken</u> him for a scarecrow striding away from a cornfield.   3

His schoolhouse stood in a lonely but pleasant spot, just at the foot of a woody hill. From there the low murmur of his pupils' voices might be heard on a drowsy summer's day like the hum of a beehive, interrupted now and then by the voice of the schoolmaster.   4

Vocabulary Questions

1. In paragraph 1, what is the meaning of the underlined word *steal*?

    A. take secretly

    B. escape

    C. commit burglary

    D. gain an extra base

    Question type 4 : **Multiple Meanings**

2. Which words from paragraph 1 most strongly suggest the sleepy nature of the valley?

    A. one of the quietest places

    B. away from the world

    C. drowsy, dreamy atmosphere

    D. spacious coves

    Question type 2 : **Context Clues**

3. Which pair of words, as used in paragraph 2, are synonyms?

    A. *dangled* and *hung*

    B. *tall* and *thin*

    C. *narrow* and *long*

    D. *schoolmaster* and *frame*

Question type (7) :**Synonyms and Antonyms**

4. In which sentence of paragraph 2 does the author use exaggeration in his description?

    A. first

    B. second

    C. third

    D. fourth

Question type (6) :**Figurative Language**

5. The word *striding* appears twice in paragraph 3. What is an antonym of *stride*?

    A. walk

    B. march

    C. pace

    D. straggle

Question type (7) :**Synonyms and Antonyms**

6. In paragraph 3, what does the underlined word profile mean?

    A. one side of the face

    B. a drawing of a facial side view

    C. information about a person

    D. outline of a land formation

Question type (4) :**Multiple Meanings**

50 ·Ten Essential Vocabulary Strategies

7. Here is a dictionary listing of the word *bag*.

   bag (bag) n. 1. sack, container. 2. purse. v. to bulge or swell. **bag and baggage** 1. with all one's possessions. 2. entirely. **left holding the bag** left with the blame. **in the bag** with success assured.

   Which definitions fit the use of the underlined word *bagging* in paragraph 3?

   A. noun

   B. verb

   C. common expressions

   D. all of above

   Question type (5) : **Dictionary Information**

8. The prefix *mis-* has different meanings in different words. Which of the following expresses the meaning it has in the word *mistaken* as it is used in paragraph 3?

   A. wrong

   B. fail

   C. hate-filled

   D. lack

   Question type (4) : **Multiple Meanings** *and*
   Question type (8) : **Affixes and Roots**

9. Which word in paragraph 4 tells you that there were trees near the schoolhouse?

   A. lonely

   B. pleasant spot

   C. woody

   D. hill

   Question type (2) : **Context Clues**

Practice for Success on Standardized Tests

10. The simile in paragraph 4 appeals to one of your senses. Which one?

    A. taste

    B. hearing

    C. touch

    D. smell

Question type **6** : **Figurative Language**

6. Essay: THE TEST OF TIME

1 How long does it take for a book to become a classic? Some say, "A generation. If parents and their children can enjoy the same story, it's a classic." Others say, "At least fifty years. A piece of writing has to stand the test of time before it can be called a classic. Only a tale with lasting appeal deserves that title."

2 It is difficult to place some classics on a time line. King Arthur, for example, is familiar to today's students through the Disney movie, *The Sword in the Stone*. However, many authors retold the story in the 1900s, starting with Howard Pyle who wrote *King Arthur and His Knights* in 1903. Much earlier, in the 1400s, Thomas Mallory collected and wrote down the Arthurian legends. Many parts of the tales have remained the same through the centuries. The presentation is what differs with each retelling. The story of King Arthur has certainly stood the test of time, but even experts cannot agree about when it first appeared.

3 It is much easier to assign dates to specific novels. *Robinson Crusoe*, written by Daniel Defoe in 1719, is recognized as a classic survival story. It was imitated in 1812 by *Swiss Family Robinson*, a book about a family (rather than an individual) that lived after their shipwreck. The genre continues to be popular. Writers of today are still producing survival novels, like Gary Paulson's *Hatchet* (1987), but only time will show if they are classics.

4 Although *Little Women* by Louisa May Alcott was written over a hundred years ago, the story remains familiar. Why? New movie _____ of the book keep appearing with new _____ playing the characters of Meg, Jo, Beth, and Amy. Movies often help to perpetuate classics.

5 The bar chart on the following page shows the length of time that a few of our many classics have been with us. The list could be ten times as long and still not contain everyone's favorites. Several of the classics listed there have been made into dramas, musicals, or movies. They have become a familiar part of our cultural heritage.

A Sampling of Classics with Their Ages

Book	Years 25–49	50–74	75–100	Over 100
Anne Frank, Diary of a Young Girl	■	■		
Dragonwings	■			
Hobbit	■	■		
Jungle Book	■	■	■	■
Little House Series	■	■	■	
Little Women	■	■	■	■
Narnia Series	■	■		
Outsiders	■			
Peter Pan	■	■	■	
Robinson Crusoe	■	■	■	■
Roll of Thunder, Hear My Cry	■			
Wizard of Oz	■	■	■	

Vocabulary Questions

1. According to the text and bar chart, how long must a book be popular for it to be described as a *classic*?

    A. fifteen years

    B. over twenty-five years

    C. fifty years

    D. over one hundred years

Question type **10** : **Pairings**

Practice for Success on Standardized Tests

2. Which words in paragraph 1 are the context clues that lead you to the meaning of the underlined word *generation*?

   A. *fifty* and *years*

   B. *book* and *classic*

   C. *test* and *time*

   D. *parents* and *children*

   Question type (2): **Context Clues**

3. About how many years is a *generation*?

   A. five to fifteen years

   B. twenty to thirty years

   C. forty to fifty years

   D. more than fifty years

   Question type (2): **Context Clues**

4. In paragraph 2, what does the underlined word *Arthurian* mean?

   A. in the kingdom

   B. long ago

   C. similar to myths

   D. about Arthur

   Question type (8): **Affixes and Roots**

5. The word *survival* appears twice in paragraph 3? What is the meaning of survival?

   A. shipwreck

   B. staying on board

   C. popular

   D. staying alive

   Question type (1): **Meaning in Sentence and Passage**

6. Which words are best for the blanks in paragraph 4?

   A. *stories* and *people*

   B. *scenes* and *girls*

   C. *versions* and *stars*

   D. *acting* and *women*

   Question type 3: **Best Words for Blanks**

7. Where do you get information about the classic, *Robinson Crusoe*?

   A. the paragraphs

   B. the chart

   C. both

   D. neither

   Question type 10: **Pairings**

8. Where do you get information about King Arthur?

   A. the paragraphs

   B. the chart

   C. both

   D. neither

   Question type 10: **Pairings**

9. Where do you get information about Mildred Taylor's classic, *Roll of Thunder, Hear My Cry*?

   A. the paragraphs

   B. the chart

   C. both

   D. neither

   Question type 10: **Pairings**

10. In the title of the chart, what does the word *sampling* mean?

   A. all classics

   B. the majority of classics

   C. favorite classics

   D. a few classics

Question type 10: **Pairings**

7. Content-Area Material: THE SEA ANEMONE

Is it a plant? Is it an animal? The sea anemone is a creature that looks more like a flower than a fish. It is <u>classified</u> with jellyfish, corals, and other "flower-like animals," but its eating behavior is anything but delicate.

1

The sea anemone is a <u>predatory</u> creature. Its tentacles keep undulating below the surface of the water, swaying like colorful plant stems. But they can be fatal to the tiny fish that swim too close to them. With a stinging shot of poison from its tentacles, the sea anemone can paralyze a fish. Then the creature nudges the helpless fish closer and closer to its round mouth until it can consume its prey.

2

The body of the sea anemone is shaped like a column with a mouth at one end and a muscular foot, or pedal disk, at the other. It can <u>adhere</u> to hard surfaces, like rocks, shells, and ship bottoms. Much of the time, a sea anemone stays stationary, firmly fixed to its base, even though it is capable of some slow movement. When strong currents threaten to <u>dislodge</u> it from its base and sweep it away, it changes its shape by pulling in its tentacles, shortening its body, and shrinking itself down to a stub.

3

Sea anemones vary greatly in size and in color. Their tentacles may be pink, blue, green, or a combination of <u>hues</u>. There are over a thousand species worldwide, and they are long-lived. So they will probably continue to puzzle people. On first sight of a sea anemone, most people ask, "Plant or animal?"

4

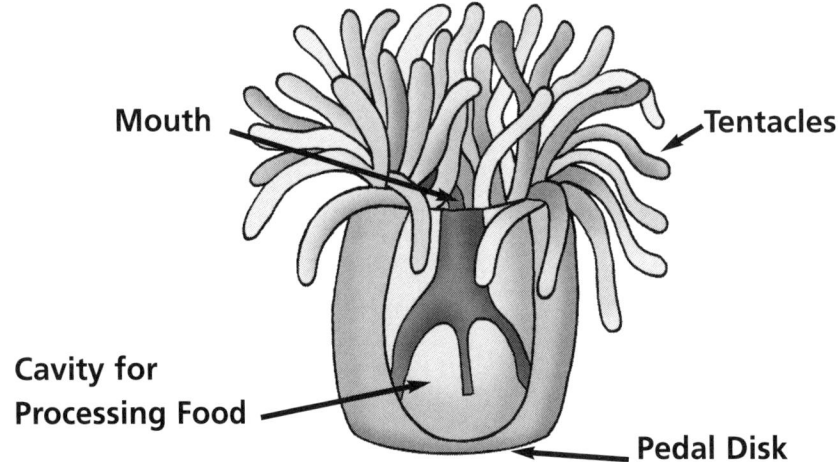

56 · Ten Essential Vocabulary Strategies

Vocabulary Questions

1. In paragraph 1, what is the meaning of the underlined word *classified*?

    A. class

    B. classes

    C. classed

    D. classification

    Question type (9): **Word Relationships**

2. In the first sentence of paragraph 2, you meet the word *predatory*. By the end of the paragraph, what meaning have you constructed for *predatory*?

    A. living underwater with tentacles

    B. stinging with poison

    C. attacking and eating other creatures

    D. paralyzing fish

    Question type (1): **Meaning in Sentence and Passage**

3. In paragraph 2, which pair of words are synonyms?

    A. *undulating* and *swaying*

    B. *poison* and *fatal*

    C. *prey* and *stems*

    D. *below* and *helpless*

    Question type (7): **Synonyms and Antonyms**

4. What word does the simile in paragraph 2 help you visualize?

    A. nudges

    B. tentacles

    C. consume

    D. creature

    Question type (6): **Figurative Language**

5. You see the words *pedal disk* in the diagram. What words in paragraph 3 give you a definition of pedal disk?

   A. some slow movement

   B. shaped like a column

   C. hard surfaces

   D. muscular foot

   Question type 10 : **Pairings**

6. Which words from paragraph 3 give you strong context clues about *stationary*?

   A. *mouth* and *body*

   B. *capable* and *rocks*

   C. *time* and *firmly*

   D. *stay* and *fixed*

   Question type 2 : **Context Clues**

7. Which meaning of *adhere* best fits the way it is used in paragraph 3?

   A. glue to, paste

   B. hold

   C. stick to, cling

   D. hug, clasp

   Question type 4 : **Multiple Meanings**

8. In paragraph 3, what is the meaning of the underlined word *dislodge*?

   A. detach

   B. attach

   C. display

   D. stub

   Question type 8 : **Affixes and Roots**

9. Which words in paragraph 4 are the strong context clues that make the meaning of the underlined word *hues* clear to you?

  A. *thousand* and *species*

  B. *pink* and *green*

  C. *combination* and *long-lived*

  D. *plant* and *animal*

Question type 2 : **Context Clues**

10. What do you learn about the tentacles from the diagram of the sea anemone?

  A. They have rounded tips.

  B. They are as thin as needles.

  C. They end in sharp points.

  D. There are just a few around the mouth.

Question type 10 : **Pairings**

8. Beliefs: MARTIN LUTHER KING JR.'S SUPPORT OF THE POOR

Martin Luther King Jr. is remembered for many reasons. He preached nonviolence. He worked for social justice, gaining the support of millions of people. He won the Nobel Peace Prize for his work in leading the African American struggle for civil rights. 1

He deserves to be remembered also as a champion of the poor. King saw that poverty created hard circumstances for people in every part of the country. In Appalachia, people were going hungry. Some Native Americans had no money for clothes for their children. Immigrants who could not yet speak English were struggling to find jobs. King knew that poverty was a problem for some African American communities, too. 2

Martin Luther King wanted to unite these people. He believed that by working together they could make a _____ by focusing the attention of the _____ on their plight. In late 1967, King started to organize a Poor People's March, which he thought would draw the attention of the country to the problem of poverty. But before the event could take place, his life was cut short. In April 1968, he was assassinated by a gunshot. 3

This champion of nonviolence faced violence many times in his life. King had been stabbed. His home had been bombed. But to the end of his life, he preached against violence and poverty. Therefore, Martin Luther King should be honored for his dual roles as a champion of nonviolence and as a supporter of the poor. 4

Practice for Success on Standardized Tests 59

Vocabulary Questions

1. You met the underlined word *nonviolence* in paragraph 1. What is an antonym of *nonviolence*?

    A. peace

    B. quiet

    C. justice

    D. violence

    Question type (7): **Synonyms and Antonyms**

2. In paragraphs 2 and 4, what is the meaning of the underlined word *champion*?

    A. defender

    B. winner

    C. fighter

    D. player

    Question type (1): **Meaning in Sentence and Passage** *and*

    Question type (4): **Multiple Meanings**

3. In paragraph 3, what is the meaning of the underlined word *focusing*?

    A. twisting the lens of a camera

    B. adjusting eye glasses

    C. bringing together rays of light

    D. directing

    Question type (4): **Multiple Meanings**

4. Which word is a synonym of *assassinated* as it is used in paragraph 3?

    A. touched

    B. killed

    C. missed

    D. wounded

    Question type (7): **Synonyms and Antonyms**

5. Which words in the passage give context clues that help you with the meaning of the underlined word *plight*?

   A. going hungry

   B. struggling to find jobs

   C. no money for clothes

   D. all of the above

   Question type ② :**Context Clues**

6. Which pair of words fits best in the blanks in paragraph 3?

   A. *difference* and *government*

   B. *march* and *prize*

   C. *noise* and *marchers*

   D. *role* and *millions*

   Question type ③ :**Best Words for Blanks**

7. Here is a dictionary listing of the word *face*.

   face (fās) n. 1. the front of the head. 2. main side or surface. v. 1. to meet with courage. 2. to turn toward.

   Which meaning fits the way the underlined word *faced* is used in paragraph 4?

   A. noun definition 1

   B. noun definition 2

   C. verb definition 1

   D. verb definition 2

   Question type ⑤ :**Dictionary Information**

8. What number is suggested by the underlined word *dual*, as it is used in paragraph 4?

   A. one

   B. two

   C. three

   D. four

   Question type ① :**Meaning in Sentence and Passage**

Practice for Success on Standardized Tests 61

9. In paragraph 4, you meet the underlined word *supporter*. In that word, what meaning does the suffix add to the root?

   A. one who

   B. more

   C. carry

   D. against

Question type 8 : **Affixes and Roots**

10. Complete this analogy:
    Rich is to *wealth* as *poor* is to

    A. hunger

    B. plight

    C. difficulty

    D. poverty

Question type 9 : **Word Relationships**

9. Graphics and Wordplay: POPULAR PUZZLES

These funny-looking word puzzles pop up everywhere—in newspapers, in magazines, even in some workbooks at school! They seem to multiply like guppies. Most people know them as "Wacky Wordies," but they have also been called "Cuckoo-Nuts" and "Patterpics." They started appearing in magazines in the late 1920s and early 1930s, and they are still going strong.   1

An airline introduced its passengers to Wacky Wordies through its magazine and challenged them to create and send in their own. The magazine was deluged. The editors said that the response was CREDJUSTIBLE (*just incredible*—"just" in "credible"). Even after the airline stopped accepting _____, more Wacky Wordies kept _____. Obviously, passengers seemed to enjoy creating them.   2

One of the most popular types of Wacky Wordies is the *position* puzzle. The statement "I understand," for example, can be represented by positioning "I" under "STAND," as follows: 3

```
┌─────────┐
│  STAND  │
│    I    │
└─────────┘
```

62 . . . . Ten Essential Vocabulary Strategies

Words that start with *over* and *under* are naturals for these graphic puzzles. *Up, down,* and *between* combinations are also easy to use. Can you figure out these Wacky Wordies?

1. BLUE / ALLS 2. WEAR / LONG 3. T O W N (vertical) 4. L L I H (vertical) 5. UJUSTS

Did you figure out *blue overalls* for the first Wacky Wordie, and *just between us* for the last one? If so, you've got the <u>hang</u> of it. Maybe you are ready to create some Wacky Wordies of your own.

Vocabulary Questions

1. The title of this selection is "Popular Puzzles." Three names for the puzzles appear in paragraph 1. Which name for them, however, appears throughout the article?

    A. Wacky Wordies

    B. Cuckoo-Nuts

    C. Patterpics

    D. all of above

    Question type **1: Meaning in Sentence and Passage**

2. What is the meaning of the expression in paragraph 1, "multiply like guppies"?

    A. reproduce in fishbowls

    B. use multiplication tables

    C. swim rapidly

    D. quickly increase in numbers

    Question type **6: Figurative Language**

3. Forms of the word *go* appear in many idioms (*going to the dogs, going back on your word, letting yourself go*). The idiom *going strong* appears at the end of paragraph 1. What does it mean?

   A. appearing frequently

   B. seldom seen

   C. ready to explode

   D. showing force

Question type **6** : **Figurative Language**

4. Which synonym of *deluged* reflects the meaning of the word in paragraph 2?

   A. underwater

   B. covered with water

   C. overwhelmed

   D. rained on heavily

Question type **7** : **Synonyms and Antonyms**

5. The affixes on the word *incredible* can help you understand it. Which definition comes closest to the meaning of the word as it is used in paragraph 2?

   A. not surprising

   B. into position

   C. unbelievable

   D. introduced

Question type **8** : **Affixes and Roots**

6. Which are the best words for the blanks in paragraph 2?

   A. *puzzles* and *composed*

   B. *words* and *writing*

   C. *passengers* and *flying*

   D. *submissions* and *arriving*

Question type **3** : **Best Words for Blanks**

7. Which synonym of *positioning* reflects the meaning of the word as it is used in paragraph 3?

   A. posing

   B. placing

   C. modeling

   D. ranking

   Question type 7 : **Synonyms and Antonyms**

8. Look back at Wacky Wordie 2 under paragraph 4. How would you read it?

   A. wear over long

   B. long underwear

   C. line between wear and long

   D. none of above

   Question type 9 : **Word Relationships** *and*

   Question type 10 : **Pairings**

9. Look back at Wacky Wordies 3 and 4 under paragraph 4. How would you read them?

   A. *downtown* and *downhill*

   B. *uptown* and *uphill*

   C. *downtown* and *uphill*

   D. *uptown* and *downhill*

   Question type 9 : **Word Relationships** *and*

   Question type 10 : **Pairings**

10. Here is a dictionary listing of the word *hang*.

hang (hang) v. 1. to fasten pictures to a wall. 2. to put to death.

get the hang of 1. to learn. 2. to understand, catch on to.

hang around 1. to cluster with others. 2. to loiter.

not give a hang about not care the least bit about.

Which line of the dictionary listing above would help you with the word *hang* as it is used in paragraph 5?

   A. line 1

   B. line 2

   C. line 3

   D. line 4

Question type 5 : **Dictionary Information**

10. Pairings: GWENDOLYN BROOKS AND PHYLLIS MCGINLEY, TWO POETS WHO WON PULITZER PRIZES

The Pulitzer Prize for poetry is a widely coveted and nationally recognized award. It has often been given to poets whose audience is adults. But two women who won the prize wrote many of their poems for children and teenagers.   1

Gwendolyn Brooks won the 1950 Pulitzer Prize for *Annie Allen*, a collection of her poems. Phyllis McGinley won in 1961 with her collection, *Times Three*. Though both females were _____ poets, they came from very different _____.   2

Brooks spent her childhood in a poor neighborhood of Chicago called Bronzeville. She used the name of her community in the titles of two of her books of verse, *A Street in Bronzeville* and *Bronzeville Boys and Girls*. Her mother, Keziah, and her father, David, encouraged Gwendolyn to write. She was only thirteen years old when her first poem was published in a magazine.   3

Though many of Phyllis McGinley's poems reflect life in and around New York City, that is not where she grew up. Her childhood was spent on a ranch in Colorado. She rode a pony to school. After her father's death, the family moved to Ogden, Utah. Like Gwendolyn Brooks, she started writing poetry when she was very young.   4

Both women were drawn to teaching. After McGinley graduated from college, she taught for a year in Utah. Then she moved to New York where she taught in a junior high school in New Rochelle. Brooks taught at several colleges. She also <u>encouraged</u> young writers by using her own money to finance prizes for elementary and high school poets.   5

Though both women wrote prose as well as poetry, they became <u>famous</u> for their verses. You may have already met poems by Gwendolyn Brooks and Phyllis McGinley in anthologies at school. Some poets say that true fame is having one's poems <u>included</u> in schoolbooks. By that definition, both of these Pulitzer Prize winners have achieved true fame.   6

Vocabulary Questions

1. In the following Venn diagram, one circle is labeled Gwendolyn Brooks. In that circle, write the words from the list that apply only to Brooks. The other circle is labeled Phyllis McGinley. In that circle, write the words that apply only to McGinley. In the center where the circles overlap, write the words that apply to both poets.

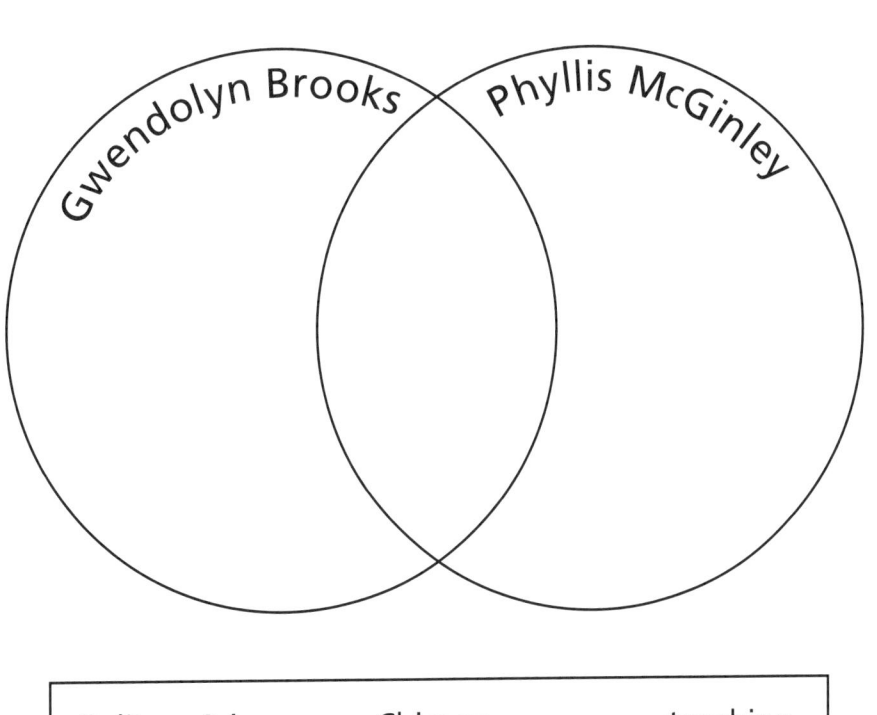

Pulitzer Prize	Chicago	teaching
New York	Bronzeville	female
	Colorado	

Question type 10 : **Pairings**

Practice for Success on Standardized Tests 67

2. In paragraph 1, you meet the underlined word *coveted*. The dictionary gives only one definition of *covet*: "to want deeply and intensely." According to that definition, how do poets feel about the Pulitzer Prize?

   A. just one more award

   B. not a very important honor

   C. some appreciation of the prize

   D. heartfelt wish to win such an honor

   Question type 5 : **Dictionary Information**

3. Which definition of *audience* fits the way the word is used in paragraph 1?

   A. people who clap in an auditorium

   B. those who pay attention to what one writes

   C. a formal meeting with an important person

   D. group assembled to hear a program

   Question type 4 : **Multiple Meanings**

4. Which pair of words fits best in the blanks in paragraph 2?

   A. *adequate* and *states*

   B. *women* and *countries*

   C. *outstanding* and *backgrounds*

   D. *winning* and *prizes*

   Question type 3 : **Best Words for Blanks**

5. Which meaning of *community* best fits the way the word is used in paragraph 3?

   A. a particular part of a city

   B. spirit of togetherness

   C. a group that has close interactions

   D. likeness, similarity

   Question type 4 : **Multiple Meanings**

6. In paragraphs 3 and 5, you meet the word *encouraged*. Which word is an antonym of *encouraged* as it is used in these paragraphs?

   A. discourteous

   B. courageous

   C. disclosed

   D. discouraged

   Question type (7): **Synonyms and Antonyms**

7. Complete this analogy:

   Poetry is to *prose* as

   A. *verses* are to *paragraphs*

   B. *rhymes* are to *punctuation*

   C. *stories* are to *characters*

   D. *words* are to *plots*

   Question type (9): **Word Relationships**

8. From its root and its suffix, what meaning do you construct for the underlined word *famous* in paragraph 6?

   A. having fame

   B. one who achieved fame

   C. more than fame

   D. believer in fame

   Question type (8): **Affixes and Roots**

9. In the word *included* in paragraph 6, which meaning does the prefix carry?

   A. not

   B. within

   C. without

   D. toward

   Question type (8): **Affixes and Roots**

Practice for Success on Standardized Tests

10. The dictionary gives only one definition of *anthology*: "a collection of poems, stories, and other writings." In which subject are you most likely to have an anthology as a schoolbook?

    A. math

    B. science

    C. social studies

    D. English

Question type 5 : **Dictionary Information**

Unit 3
MORE PRACTICE on
vocabulary through wordplay

Wordplay is a great way to extend your vocabulary. Let's have fun as we look at some of the word work you did in the first two units.

Here are some ways to revisit synonyms, idioms, analogies, multiple meanings, unusual word relationships, and other topics related to the top ten types of vocabulary questions. On these activity pages, you will find that building your vocabulary through wordplay is fun.

1. The Stronger Synonym
2. Idioms, Featuring Wacky Wordies
3. Ana-Pal Pairs
4. Double Definitions
5. Analogy Puzzle

THE STRONGER SYNONYM

Some synonyms are stronger than others. *Beautiful* is stronger than *pretty*. *Hideous* is stronger than *ugly*. To answer each question below, write the stronger synonym. If you are not sure, check a dictionary.

1. Which building is larger—the *big* one or the *tremendous* one? _____

2. Which is a worse mistake—an *error* or a *blunder*? _____

3. Would a comedian rather be called *funny* or *hilarious*? _____

4. Would hungry people refer to themselves as *empty* or *famished*? _____

5. Which person is worse—a *scoundrel* or a *rascal*? _____

6. Would a smart student rather be called *bright* or *brilliant*? _____

7. Which room looks worse—an *untidy* room or a *messy* room? _____

8. Which person is nosey—a *snoopy* person or a *curious* person? _____

9. Would you call an enraged person *indignant* or *infuriated*? _____

10. Would you refer to someone's wrongdoing as a *villainy* or a *foible*? _____

11. Which applause is louder—the one that *resounds* or the one that *deafens*?

    _____

12. Who is deliberately mean—a *vicious* person or an *inconsiderate* person?

    _____

13. Who is the better speaker—the *orator* or the *chatterer*? _____

14. Which child is better-behaved—a *cherub* or an *imp*? _____

15. Which look lasts longer—a *glance* or a *gaze*? _____

16. Which book has more pages—a *voluminous* one or a *thick* one? _____

IDIOMS, FEATURING WACKY WORDIES

When you want to express the idea "angry," you have a lot of choices. The word has many synonyms, ranging from *displeased* to *furious*. Also there are many idioms that carry the idea of "angry." Look at *flaring up, flying into a rage,* and *getting hot under the collar.*

Idioms use figurative language to express meaning. Word-by-word reading of an idiom won't help you figure it out. You need to learn the meaning of the whole expression.

Quite a few idioms can be represented as Wacky Wordies. You can read this one as "hot under the collar."

Look at these Wackie Wordies. On the line that goes with each one, write the idiom that it represents. Then, write what the idiom means.

Idiom   **Meaning**

1. _____   _____

2. _____   _____

3. _____   _____

4. _____   _____

1. LO [HEAD/HEELS] VE

2. TALKING / YOUR K HAT (with TALKING vertical through HAT)

3. THE WEATHER / FEELING

4. D E F (vertical)

Practice for Success on Standardized Tests 73

Idiom	Meaning
5. _____	_____
6. _____	_____
7. _____	_____
8. _____	_____
9. _____	_____

5. `HISROPEHE'S`

6. `SKINNED`

7. `HANDED`

8. `THEIT'SBAG`

9. `ENDSENDS` (vertical)

ANA-PAL PAIRS

Some words are exactly the same when spelled forward and backward. Look at *mom, peep,* and *radar.* These words are called palindromes.

Some pairs of words contain the same letters, but in different order. Look at *ape* and *pea, meat* and *mate, stove* and *votes, finger* and *fringe.* These pairs are called anagrams.

The words that you will list below contain the same letters. The letters, forward and backward, spell two different words. Examples: *tub* and *but, tang* and *gnat, pools* and *sloop.* These pairs of words are a bit like anagrams and a bit like palindromes. That's why we call them *Ana-Pal Pairs*.

Use the clues to fill in each pair.

1. ___ ___ ___ short sleep

   ___ ___ ___ utensil for frying

2. ___ ___ ___ number before eleven

   ___ ___ ___ for catching fish

3. ___ ___ ___ at the present time

   ___ ___ ___ came in first

4. ___ ___ ___ a noisy dance

   ___ ___ ___ a gentle touch

5. ___ ___ ___ ___ basic part of a house

   ___ ___ ___ ___ marshy wasteland

6. ___ ___ ___ ___ forest animal

   ___ ___ ___ ___ hollow stem of grass

7. ___ ___ ___ ___ ___ skins of fruits

   ___ ___ ___ ___ ___ slumber

Practice for Success on Standardized Tests

8. __ __ __ __ __ narrow strip, belt

   __ __ __ __ __ not wholes

9. __ __ __ __ __ __ prize given for merit

   __ __ __ __ __ __ part of a dresser that can be pulled out and pushed in

10. __ __ __ __ __ __ __ __ treats at the end of a meal

    __ __ __ __ __ __ __ __ feeling the pressure

DOUBLE DEFINITIONS

To a lawyer, *court* is an indoor place to work. To a tennis pro, *court* is an outdoor place to play the game. Many common words get different definitions from different people.

Write the definition you think each person would give for the featured word. (The first one is done for you.)

1. What are *tracks*?

   Answer from a railroad engineer: <u>rails for a train's wheels</u>

   Answer from a forest ranger: <u>footprints of an animal</u>

2. What is a *page*?

   Answer from an editor: _____

   Answer from a senator: _____

3. What is a *bug*?

   Answer from an exterminator: _____

   Answer from a computer programmer: _____

4. What is a *reel*?

   Answer from owner of a fishing boat: _____

   Answer from director of a movie: _____

5. What is an *anchor*?

   Answer from a sailor: _____

   Answer from a television producer: _____

6. What is a *scale*?

   Answer from a grocer: _____

   Answer from a musician: _____

7. What is a *crane*?

   Answer from a bird-watcher: _____

   Answer from a builder: _____

8. What is a *meter*?

   Answer from a math teacher: _____

   Answer from a police officer: _____

9. What is a *case*?

   Answer from a social worker: _____

   Answer from a luggage salesperson: _____

10. What is a *crook*?

    Answer from a shepherd: _____

    Answer from a judge: _____

ANALOGY PUZZLE

Here is a shortcut to writing an analogy:

    day : night :: light : dark

You can read that analogy as "*Day* is to *night* as *light* is to *dark*."

Below are the first two words in ten analogies. They show the relationship you want to duplicate for the last two words. Beware—some are tricky wordplay relationships.

In the following box are twenty words you can use to complete the analogies. Be ready to erase. You may change your mind a few times as you fill in the blanks.

air	eye	hill	perch
bay	fawns	jay	ram
danger	fish	lever	revel
does	half	mountain	safety
ewe	heir	one	water

1. river : stream :: _____ : _____

2. wild : tame :: _____ : _____

3. rooster : chicken :: _____ : _____

4. dew : do :: _____ : _____

5. quart : pint :: _____ : _____

6. wolf : flow :: _____ : _____

7. swallow : bird :: _____ : _____

8. bee : sea :: _____ : _____

9. colts : mares :: _____ : _____

10. land : peninsula :: _____ : _____